T0209279

To purchase the companion C.D. you may order it on line
or from Ruth LaFreniere at nanalala4031@icloud.com

Stories, Psalms, and Songs for the Darkest Night

Hope and Help for Surviving Depression

Ruth LaFreniere

WESTBOW
P R E S S®
A DIVISION OF THOMAS NELSON
& ZONDERVAN

THE HOLY BIBLE, NEW INTERNATIONAL VERSION®, NIV® Copyright © 1973,
1978, 1984, 2011 by Biblica, Inc.® Used by permission. All rights reserved worldwide.

Scripture quotations marked (NLT) are taken from the Holy Bible,
New Living Translation, copyright © 1996, 2004, 2007 by Tyndale
House Foundation. Used by permission of Tyndale House Publishers,
Inc., Carol Stream, Illinois 60188. All rights reserved.

Scripture taken from the King James Version of the Bible.

The Living Bible copyright © 1971 by Tyndale House Foundation. Used
by permission of Tyndale House Publishers Inc., Carol Stream, Illinois
60188. All rights reserved. The Living Bible, TLB, and the The Living
Bible logo are registered trademarks of Tyndale House Publishers.

Scripture taken from The Message. Copyright © 1993, 1994, 1995, 1996,
2000, 2001, 2002. Used by permission of NavPress Publishing Group.

This book is a work of non-fiction. Unless otherwise noted, the author and the publisher
make no explicit guarantees as to the accuracy of the information contained in this book
and in some cases, names of people and places have been altered to protect their privacy.

WestBow Press books may be ordered through booksellers or by contacting:

WestBow Press
A Division of Thomas Nelson & Zondervan
1663 Liberty Drive
Bloomington, IN 47403
www.westbowpress.com
1 (866) 928-1240

Because of the dynamic nature of the Internet, any web addresses or links contained in
this book may have changed since publication and may no longer be valid. The views
expressed in this work are solely those of the author and do not necessarily reflect the
views of the publisher, and the publisher hereby disclaims any responsibility for them.

Any people depicted in stock imagery provided by Getty Images are models,
and such images are being used for illustrative purposes only.
Certain stock imagery © Getty Images.

ISBN: 978-1-9736-5520-6 (sc)
ISBN: 978-1-9736-5519-0 (hc)
ISBN: 978-1-9736-5521-3 (e)

Library of Congress Control Number: 2019902704

Print information available on the last page.

WestBow Press rev. date: 02/21/2020

Contents

Foreword

Are You Depressed, Afraid, Alone?

You are not alone!
Today Christians who are hurting often wear their masks tightly in place to disguise the pain.

There is hope and help. You can start today on a new path to bring healing to your mind and spirit.

Here is a journey of a simple faith in a big God who made all the difference for Ruth. Emergency brain surgery left her with a one-sided paralysis, an unwanted divorce, a significant music career loss, and a depression that caused her to question whether God was even there for her or cared about her struggles.

R uth LaFreniere is a professional musician who knows that God is the God of second chances. She and her husband, Paul, share their story through music and the Word at churches, retreats, and conferences around the country. They also entertain at senior retirement communities, resorts, fairs, weddings, and celebrations with jazz.

Paul is a professional trumpet player. He recently had most of his right lung removed due to cancer. It has not affected his masterful playing at all!

Preface

Depression. We've all experienced it. It can be short-lived; it is for many people when circumstances of life are difficult.

But what about depression that goes on and on? The kind that leaves you paralyzed and unable to function—depression that leaves you hopeless?

Clinical depression (caused by a chemical imbalance in the brain) requires medical attention and medication.

I have clinical depression and take medication. As a Christian, I believe God is willing to help me as I do my part on my journey of life.

Ruthie LaFreniere

When I'm Depressed,
I Feel Ugly

The Beauty of the Lord

Let the beauty of the Lord be upon us and
establish the work of our hands.
—Psalm 90:17 (KJV)

April 1983. I've just come home from the hospital after a two-and-a-half-month stay following brain surgery. I stand here in front of a full-length mirror and stare at my body—a body that looks so different from the one I knew. Before surgery, I was a tiny size 3. But I have gained nearly thirty pounds!

My left side is paralyzed and droops downward. Part of my head has been shaved, and my hair is merely short stubble. My face is swollen from the medications.

I stare at this unfamiliar image and cry out, "Oh, Lord, there is no outward beauty left! You've got to help me become beautiful on the inside."

God is giving me beauty lessons as I immerse myself in His Word and spend time in conversation with Him. Slowly, He is washing away the ugliness within. He is rinsing away anger, resentment, pride, and jealousy and replacing them with the beauty of Himself—grace, forgiveness, humility, and love.

It's a daily task, but what a trade-off!

Recognizing the Symptoms

- Lack of personal hygiene
- Unhealthy eating habits
- Comparing your looks to others

Taking Positive Steps

- Shower or bathe and wash your face every day. Get dressed. Comb your hair.
- Avoid junk food. Drink plenty of water. Eat a good breakfast.

When I'm Depressed,
I Feel Exhausted

I'm Flying With Wings

They that wait upon the Lord shall renew their strength.
They shall mount up with wings like eagles. They shall
run and not be weary, they shall walk and not faint.

—Isaiah 40:31 (TLB)

My father went home to be with his Lord in February 1982. That very day, I decided to change my life's verse to the one he had chosen forty years earlier: Isaiah 40:31. I had no idea what the implications of that choice would be. One year and nine days later, I was in a holding pattern—waiting on the Lord in new ways.

It is May 1983. Following brain surgery, I am left paralyzed on one side of my body, unable to walk. My life as I knew it has come to a screeching halt. I am unable to care for my young daughters. And folding clothes, cooking, sweeping floors, washing my hair, and playing the piano—all with one hand—seem impossible.

My daily life has become painfully slow in contrast to the fast pace I was used to. Now I spend my time learning to make a bed, wash the dishes, fold fitted sheets, iron, and even put on pierced earrings with those tiny little backs!

But I am waiting also for God to physically heal me, emotionally strengthen me, and spiritually grow me.

I am continually being spiritually renewed. I am walking, running, and even flying with Yahweh because I'm waiting on Him to feed me and renew my soul. There are times when I falter and experience doubts. Then I stop and wait on the Lord. He renews my strength, and soon I'm soaring above the storms of life!

Recognizing the Symptoms

- Sluggish; a slowing down of metabolism
- Unable to do household chores

Taking Positive Steps

- Get outside and walk around the block or yard. Oxygen to the brain is a must. Energy begets energy. Eat regular meals. Delegate responsibilities. Ask for help.

When I'm Depressed,
I Feel Confused

Trust in God

Trust God from the bottom of your heart; don't
try to figure out everything on your own.
Listen for God's voice in everything you do, everywhere
you go; He's the one who will keep you on track.
Don't assume you know it all. Run to God. Run
from evil! Your body will glow with health!
Your very bones will vibrate with life!
Honor God in everything you do.
—Proverbs 3:5–7 (The Message)

June 1983. My friends and family probably would best describe me as self-sufficient, independent, knowledgeable, and analytical. I'm not afraid of anyone or anything. In fact, I'm feisty.

I'm also the kind of person who seems to have the answer to everything.

These are descriptions of me before brain surgery left me partially paralyzed.

How quickly my world has changed.

Now I find I'm dependent on everyone. My husband and children have to help me with everything from getting dressed, to using the bathroom, to cutting the meat on my plate.

Now I have *no* answers, only questions. How will I deal with this sudden change in my life? Will I learn to walk again? Will I regain the use of my left hand? Why has this happened?

There are no pat answers. I can't figure this out on my own.

I *have* to trust God for the future. But especially, I am learning how to trust Him for every single moment of each day.

Recognizing the Symptoms

- Doubting your faith/beliefs

Taking Positive Steps

- Affirm your faith out loud (e.g., "I believe God loves me").
- Turn off the TV and listen to good music.
- Write affirmative scriptures on three-by-five cards and tape them to the mirror, refrigerator, etc.

When I'm Depressed,

I Feel Bitter and Negative

It is Good to Praise You, Lord

It is good to praise you, Lord, to proclaim your love
in the morning and your faithfulness at night.
For you make me glad by your deeds, O Lord.
I sing for joy at the works of your hand.

—Psalm 2:1–2, 4 (NIV)

S eptember 1985. You would think that being paralyzed would be the worst possible tragedy in my life. You see, I had been a concert pianist, and now my left hand is limp and useless.

But two years later, I face a much greater loss. My marriage of sixteen years is over. My two teenage daughters and I are on our own. As far as I am concerned, I have a huge F on my report card of life, and it is also tattooed on my forehead.

"This is more than I can bear!" I cry. "Surely God cannot use me anymore."

Reading through the psalms each day, I am faced with the word *praise* over and over again. How does one praise God in the midst of tragedy? Doesn't it seem absurd, even hypocritical? But there it is: praise.

After reading these verses many times, I realize that I can praise God for His love. He is faithful to me even when others are not. His deeds are worthy of praise.

Praise is a matter of the will, not emotion. As a friend of mine says, "Praise God *until* you feel like it—not just *when* you feel like it.

The result of praising God? He makes me glad.

Recognizing the Symptoms

- Reciting to others all the bad things that have happened to you
- Holding grudges and anger
- Thinking others are more successful than you

Taking Positive Steps

- Each day, write down (or say out loud) at least one thing or person you are thankful for.
- Each day, write down (or say out loud) at least one quality or attribute of God you are thankful for, such as His love, power, and forgiveness.

When I'm Depressed,
I Feel Brokenhearted

You Fill me with Joy

Lord, you have assigned me my portion and
my cup; you have made my lot secure.
The boundary lines have fallen for me in pleasant places.
You have made known to me the path of life;
you will fill me with joy in your presence.
—Psalm 16:5–6, 11(NIV)

June 1995. I have just flown from Salem, Oregon, to London, England, to visit family. I'm so excited because I've never been overseas before. I plan to stay for one month and have a huge suitcase to prove it! Now everything has gone horribly wrong, and I need to leave. I find myself all alone in a foreign country with my huge suitcase, a shoulder bag, and a cane in my only functioning hand. And I am sixty miles from the airport.

It was difficult, but I've finally made it to London, and I'm waiting for a flight on standby.

Three days later, I'm finally on my way back to the States. Through tears of pain and sorrow, I search the scriptures for some words of comfort. In the first two verses of Psalm 16, David cried out for God to keep him safe, wanting the refuge of his Lord. This seems appropriate.

But then I read further. "You fill me with joy." Now here is a promise. I don't have to muster up some joy. David says God filled him with joy. I am so blessed by this good news that I write a song as we fly over the Atlantic.

Believe me: God can fill you too with joy right now—no matter how difficult your circumstances appear to be.

Recognizing the Symptoms

- Unable to find humor—or anything—to smile about in daily life

Taking Positive Steps

- Read the psalms.
- Read the comics.
- Watch Christian comedies.

When I'm Depressed,
I Feel Alone

Like a Shepherd

When you pass through the waters, I will be with you; and when you pass through the rivers, they will not sweep over you. When you walk through the fire, you will not be burned.

—Isaiah 43:2–3 (NIV)

April 1996. I have just walked away from my second marriage. I can't take my husband's anger anymore. My first marriage ended because of abuse, and now I'm reliving the nightmare. How did this happen? I'm so humiliated. What will my friends think?

All my belongings are in storage, and I'm house-sitting—moving from place to place. I'm over fifty; I'm disabled; I have no job, and I'm all alone. I'm also angry with myself, my husband, and even God.

Now, as I lie here in this strange bed in an unfamiliar house, familiar words from the Old Testament come to my mind. (I'm grateful I memorized scripture in my youth.) These words are found in Isaiah 43:2–3.

Still more words come to mind—now from an old hymn. "Neither life nor death can ever, from the Lord, His children sever."

I'm not alone. Jesus is right here with me, surrounding me with His love and care. Now I will surround myself with loving friends and church family to sustain me through this ordeal. In Jesus I am secure.

He will feed His flock like a shepherd. He will carry the lambs in His arms, holding them close to His heart. Isaiah 40:11 NLT

Recognizing the Symptoms

- Lack of social life, cutting off friends, and skipping functions, church, and shopping

Taking Positive Steps

- Call someone every day or ask a friend or family member to check on you.
- Choose one event or function to attend every week.

When I'm Depressed,

I Feel Empty

O How He Loves You and Me

My thoughts trouble me and I am distraught.
My heart is in anguish within me, the
terrors of death assail me.
Fear and trembling have beset me. But I
call to God and the Lord saves me.
Evening, morning and noon I cry out in
distress and He hears my voice.
—Psalm 55:4a, 5, 16

Jesus, I Come to Thee
Out of my bondage, sorrow and night
Jesus, I come; Jesus, I come.
Into Thy freedom, gladness and light
Jesus, I come to Thee.
Out of my sickness into Thy health;
Out of my want and into Thy wealth.
Out of my sin and into Thyself,
Jesus, I come to Thee.

It is the summer of 1999, and I am in a place I have never been to before. It is beyond the bottom of the pit. Throughout the past eighteen years, since my brain surgery, I have dealt with tough stuff and struggled with depression. But this is a different depression. I am doubting God's presence, His love—actually His existence. I sit here in my living room with the drapes closed and feel completely empty. I want to go to sleep and never wake up.

Several days have now passed, and I realize this feeling is not going to go away for a while. Intellectually, I know all the answers, but they mean nothing to me. I've decided to just live in my depression, and to believe that if there is a God, He will just have to take me the way I am.

I am finally beginning to feel His presence. Little by little, I am able to reach out to Him with tiny baby steps. As I come to Jesus with my despair and sorrow, He is leading me into peace, confidence, and, yes, joy.

Recognizing the Symptoms

- Trying to be "up" for everyone and denying your depression

Taking Positive Steps

- Share your depression with a trusted friend.
- Go ahead and cry.
- Write a letter to God and tell Him your feelings.

When I'm Depressed,
I Feel Afraid

Under the Shadow of His Wings

Those who live in the shelter of the Most
High will find rest in the Almighty.
He will shield you with His wings. He
will shelter you with His feathers.
—Psalm 91:1, 4 (NLT)

I was privileged to grow up in a minister's home. I say "privileged" because I was exposed to the scriptures on a daily basis. Each night Daddy would call us together around the fireplace in the living room for devotions. Sometimes he would read to us from *Pilgrim's Progress*; often we would memorize scripture verses, but mostly we would take turns reading from the Holy Bible.

My mother tells me that when I was six years old, I memorized several verses in Psalm 91. I had trouble pronouncing all the words in the King James Bible we used—words such as pestilence, habitation, and buckler. But I understood the meaning of them and knew that God was my protection and that I didn't need to stay afraid. He would take away my fear because I knew He sheltered me.

I have long forgotten most of the verses in chapter 91, but I still remember verse one. What a comfort it has been to me through the years—and it still is, fifty years later.

Recognizing the Symptoms

- Afraid of the unknown
- Afraid of making decisions

Taking Positive Steps

- Memorize a scripture verse.

When I'm Depressed,
I Feel Defeated

Benediction

May the Lord answer you in distress. May
He send you help from His sanctuary.
May He give you the desires of your heart
and make all your plans succeed.
We will shout for joy when you are victorious and
will lift up our banner to the name of our God.
—Psalm 20:1–2, 45 (NIV)

Distress. We all experience it. Pain, disappointment, rejection, and fear are part of our daily lives.

There are many times when I feel so alone and so hopeless that I do not have the energy to pray. I can only lie on my bed and whisper, "Help."

God has brought me help, sometimes through a phone call, a visit from a friend, or the recollection of a comforting Bible verse. But more often through just a tiny ray of hope. A small amount of faith. A thin thread of assurances that He, the God of the universe, hears my cries and is sending help.

In my broken, helpless state, I want more than anything else to be useful to God. This has always been my desire. Not only has He fulfilled that desire, He gives me new desires. My wants begin to conform to God's wants; His plans are becoming my plans.

Since they are His plans, He is allowing me to succeed and experience victory.

Pain and rejection will always come and go. That's the reality of life. God sends us help, and we can succeed when we allow Him to have control of our lives.

Recognizing the Symptoms

- Feeling guilty about past decisions

Taking Positive Steps

- Stop asking "why" and saying "if only."
- Post scripture verses about God's love and faithfulness around the house or office.

When I'm Depressed,
I Feel Victimized

Grace

My grace is enough; it's all you need.
My strength comes into its own in your weakness.
—2 Corinthians 12:9 (The Message)

When I experience difficult times in my life, this verse reminds me that God's grace is enough to walk me through the deep waters or the raging fires (Isaiah 43:2). But when trouble first surfaces, I only feel discouragement, disbelief, and despair.

Over the last fifteen years, I have become physically challenged, gone through a divorce, seen my youngest daughter give birth to a child at age seventeen, lost the close relationship of my daughters and family members, dealt with the death of a stepson, experienced the death of my father, and been diagnosed with clinical depression and posttraumatic stress syndrome. There are times when I feel such sorrow and loss that it is easy to fall into the role of a victim.

This is not what I had planned for my life.

In my young adulthood, I thought that when everything settled down—all the tough stuff was taken care of—I could "get on with life."

But life is not a rehearsal. Everything that happens *is* life and is what makes me who I am. In the midst of my weakest moments, I know that God's strength can overcome my frailties. His grace *is* enough to handle all of my sorrows.

By God's grace, I can stand before Him and give to Him all the heartaches, all the failures, and all the disappointments of life. Thankfully it's not my human endeavors that allow me into His presence, but His grace alone that makes me worthy.

Recognizing the Symptoms

- Comparing your circumstance to that of others

Taking Positive Steps

- Volunteer at a rescue mission, church, boys' and girls' club, hospital, or other local social organization. It will help you put your problems into perspective.

When I'm Depressed,

I Will Worship God

*Majesty, How Majestic is Your Name,
O Worship the King, O Could I Speak*

O Lord, our Lord, how majestic is your name in all the earth!
—Psalm 8:1

Thirty years have come and gone filled with ups and downs. I haven't physically fallen very often in that time, but when I do, it is devastating! I feel so vulnerable.

After one particular fall the Holy Spirit gently reminded me that I am falling at the feet of Jesus. That changes my perspective; I am no longer feeling sorry for myself but am worshipping God.

Worship isn't just for Sundays. When we think, say, and do all things for the glory of God, we are worshipping Him; however, we can take time each day for bowing before Him in worship.

Psalm 99:5 says, "Exalt the Lord our God! Bow low before his feet, for he is holy!" (NLT).

Majesty

Majesty, worship his majesty.
Unto Jesus be all glory, power and praise.
Majesty, kingdom authority flow from his throne
Unto his own his anthem raise
So exalt, lift up on high the name of Jesus.
Magnify, come glorify Christ Jesus the King.
Jesus who died, now glorified,
King of all kings.

—Jack W. Hayford

When I'm Depressed,
I Will Pray

Father, I Adore You

Don't worry about anything; instead pray about everything. Tell God what you need, and thank him for all he has done.

NLT

I believe praying is vital to our relationship with God. It is simply talking with Him and then listening for His "voice." Too often we go to God with our "grocery list" when what He really wants is communion with us.

I use a three-prong form of prayer: First, I praise and thank Him; second, I confess my sins; and third, I intercede for others and then for myself.

Prayer (especially intercessory) takes my mind off myself and puts it on my Heavenly Father.

Father, I Adore You
Father, I adore you; lay my life before you.
How I love you.

Jesus, I adore you; lay my life before you.
How I love you.

Spirit, I adore you; lay my life before you.
How I love you.
—Terrye Coelho

When I'm Depressed,
I Will Let God Lead Me

He Leadeth Me

I, being in the way, the lord led me.

—Genesis 24:27 (KJV)

I have always been fiercely independent. Just ask my family and friends. Being independent and tenacious has helped me as I've struggled through the years. But it can also get me into trouble if I don't allow God to lead me. Sometimes I forge my own path instead of following the Shepherd.

An old hymn expresses my desire to let God lead me.

> He leadeth me, he leadeth me.
> By his own hand he leadeth me.
> His faithful follower I would be,
> For by his hand he leadeth me.
>
> —Joseph Gilmore

Psalm 48:17 reads, "This is what the Lord says, 'I am the Lord your God who teaches you what is good for you and leads you along the paths you should follow'" (NLT).

When I'm Depressed,
I Will Be a Witness of God's Grace

Shine, Jesus, Shine

For you are to be his witness, telling everyone
what you have seen and heard.
—Acts 1:8 (NLT)

This may seem elementary, even silly, but I asked the Lord to put a smile on my face. You see, I used to be quite serious and seldom smiled. I was a perfectionist and disliked it when things didn't go my way.

Now He has put a smile on my face, and people are so blest by it. It's a witness to all who see me and gives me opportunities to share my faith with them.

When I'm Depressed,
I Will Walk by Faith

I Want Jesus To Walk With Me

We walk by faith and not by sight.
—2 Corinthians 5:7 (KJV)

I find it interesting that the first time I was able to sing a solo after my brain surgery, I chose a song entitled "Walk'n in the Light of his Love."

I could barely walk and was using a cane or a wheelchair! Singing that song was an act of faith on my part.

As we walk this journey here on earth, it is essential that we acknowledge Jesus's presence in our lives. Although we can't see Him, by faith we believe He is ever-present.

When I'm Depressed,

I Will Share My Needs with Someone

Walking Crookedly

Share each other's burdens, and in this
way obey the law of Christ.
—Galations 6:2 (NLT)

I remember soon after my month-long stay in the hospital, people at church would come up to me and tell me they were praying for my healing. With expectancy on their face, they would ask me if I was better—were their prayers working? Not wanting to disappoint them, I would smile and say yes.

But I wasn't. It was hard to be transparent. I needed to be honest and bare my soul to someone I trusted. It took me awhile, but I finally did just that. We all need someone with whom we can share our burdens.

The blind musician Ken Medea has written a song that asks the question, "If this is not a place where my heart-cries can be heard, where can I go to cry?" The "place" he is speaking of is the body of Christ. Let's be willing to find a friend, a family member, or a pastor, take off our masks and share our heart-cries.

When I'm Depressed,

I Will Hope in the Lord

A Journey of Hope

I pray that God, the source of hope, will fill you completely with joy and peace because you trust in Him. Then you will overflow with confident hope through the power of the Holy Spirit.

—Romans 15:13 (NLT)

This is not the "crossing my fingers" kind of hope that says, "I hope it doesn't rain." My hope is in God, my Heavenly Father.

I am so thankful that I learned scripture verses as a child. With the help of the Holy Spirit I'm able to recall those verses, and they give me such hope. Why? Because the Word of God is true, and the power of the Holy Spirit is available to me all the time.

Postscript

It Is Well with My Soul

Praise be to God... who works out everything in conformity to the purpose of His will... in order that we might be to the praise of His glory.
Ephesians 1:3, 11–12

The Christian walk is a paradox. It is a journey of tears, pain, and sorrow, yet also one of joy, victory, and hope. The struggles of life have caused me to run to the arms of Jesus. In His presence I find comfort, strength, and joy. Nothing in this world can compare to Him. He is truly my best friend.

Thankfully, God has healed my marriage. We continue to experience His grace in our lives. God uses us in spite of ourselves! 2 Corinthians 8:12 sums it all up: "For if the willingness is there the gift is acceptable according to what one has, not according to what one does not have."

May we willingly surrender the circumstances of our lives and choose joy in the midst of pain, and experience a journey of hope.

> When peace like a river attendeth my way.
> When sorrows like sea billows roll;
> Whatever my lot thou hast taught me to say,
> "It is well, it is well with my soul."
> —Horacio Spafford

Printed in the United States
By Bookmasters